Communion

To Gill
Something of an earthly
Communion, but
Sacred all the same!

Deborah Harvey

Deborah

27th June 2011

Indigo Dreams Publishing

First Edition: Communion
First published in Great Britain in 2011 by:
Indigo Dreams Publishing
132 Hinckley Road
Stoney Stanton
Leicestershire
LE9 4LN

www.indigodreams.co.uk

ISBN 978-1-907401-51-0
British Library Cataloguing in Publication Data. A CIP record for this book can be obtained from the British Library.

Designed and typeset in Palatino Linotype by Indigo Dreams.

Cover design by Ronnie Goodyer at Indigo Dreams. Cover photograph of mural at St Winifred's, Branscombe and three hares illustration ©Dru Marland.

Printed and bound in Great Britain by Imprint Academic, Exeter.

For HH,
Poet

Acknowledgements

Some of these poems have been previously published by Beehive Press, Cinnamon Press, Leaf Books, Mslexia, Poetry Can, Poetry Now, Poetry Space, Ragged Raven, Salopeot, Writer's Forum.

Coleridge Changes his Library Books won the 2010 Wells International Poetry Competition. *The Mary Block* and *Public Transport* were highly commended in the 2010 Poetry Space Competition. *The Red of His Coat* won second prize in the 2008 Yeovil Literary Prize and *Prawle Point* was highly commended in the 2009 Yeovil Literary Prize. *Remedy* won third prize in the 2008 Essex Poetry Festival Competition. *Redcliffe* won the 2000 Pulsar Poetry Prize. *The Gatekeeper* was specially commended in the 2009 Welsh Poetry Competition. *Kin* won the 2011 Dor Kemmyn Poetry Competition. *Poem for a Final Anniversary* won second prize in the 2010 Rhyme and Reason Poetry Competition. *Dragonfly* was highly commended in the 2000 Linkway Poetry Competition. *Clearing from the West* won second prize in Writers' Forum Competition in July 2001. *The Wedding Tree* was commended in the 2009 Mslexia Poetry Competition.

With thanks to Kate Dunn and Reg Meuross.

CONTENTS

Communion

Tobruk

Silence,
not for two minutes
but sixty years.

Only then does he start to talk,
not to his family, but his brothers,
those soldiers in slippers,
with cemetery teeth,
their medals saucepan lids
pinned to punctured chests,
their stories shrapnel
lodged in matter
from a distant land called War.

Later I gather rusted splinters,
their gist a desert expedition:
mirage of wire;
signs in barbed Gothic script;
hot metal surfacing
through oceanic sand, in front, behind. I panic,
turn to trace his steps,
a trail of breadcrumbs
swallowed up by circling dunes,

not knowing how this terror ends,
if my father will survive
to speak its name.

Nettle Rash

Every now and then
I get out the milk pan
to make junket,
warming the milk and the rennet
to the temperature of blood,
then letting it thicken and cool.
Barely set and freckled with nutmeg,

its taste conjures
moon daisies, drowsy peonies,
a windfall of laughter and stories
in apple-deep shadows,
licking fingers,
sticky with raspberries
and bottled cream,

and the memory of you,
tracing the nettle rash
staining the milkiness of my skin,
in the treacherous depths
of our thicket bed,
our lips stung with kisses,
our quickening breath.

Coleridge Changes His Library Books

All this altering year you've called me
from the hills above Nether Stowey,
in the shifting of fossils and siltstones
that clutter Kilve's wilderness shore. In Porlock
I glimpsed you through watered windows
at the hearth of the mariners' inn
with jugfuls of cider, potted laver,
a communion of friends.

I saw your whole world imaged at Wyndcliff,
a moss-softened step for each day
that I gazed upon a Xanadu made real,
from the mazy ramblings of the Wye
down to a sunless Severn Sea.
Even the swift, sleek-whiskered river,
baptising the churchtown of your birth,
floated a dream of you

in a nutshell with paper sails,
walking your poems down droves and causeways,
lugging your library books forty miles,
till Bristol lights its tide of stars
and I see you
brimming with words and stories
all along the Hotwells Road,
as high as the swifts that scream over our city.

Communion

for MFT

She lifts her veil of lace,
her eyes are narrowed and her face
upturned for kisses,

and as she draws her lover in,
he binds her close
with promises. Yes,

they will prey,
but on each other
on this holy feasting day.

They don't appear
to feel the Devil's spear
thrust into their sides,

don't realise
that they're a warning
painted on this ancient wall

to a score of generations
against temptations
of the flesh. Instead,

they'll partake of each other
in red mouths of sandstone spires,
in sumptuous, honey-coloured quires,

in sanctuary, chapter house and chantry,
once used as store for vestments,
warm with candlelight and incense,

in drowned and sinking chapels
filling up with sand and lapped
by worn stone steps.

In sacred glades and nymets
beneath the fan-vaulting of trees,
she'll smile and slither to her knees

on mossy hassocks, last year's leaves,
like her dress of lovat silk
snagged on a hook.

*In St Winifred's Church, Branscombe, Devon, a mural of 1450 warns
against Lust.*

Motherlode

Her body a body of water,
running slack after the storm
and oceanic,
its surface mapped and moulded
like the scrolling print of waves
on sprawling sandflats,

yet as mountainous as the rock
to which Prometheus was bound,
weighing her down, fixing her
inextricably
in this small life she has surrendered
and made smaller.

These sacred days
with their tidal rhythms
and the symmetry of wheat
are pinned and worked
with tiny stitches,
barely noticed.

Plainsong

for TCH

I was bringing in the washing,
folding laundered clothes and bedding,
all woven with the warmth of early summer,
when I noticed the new leaves on the creeper,
how in their gleaming
they were the colours of carnival glass.

That night the rain in the crab apple tree,
the plainsong of ring doves
and thinking of you kept me from sleeping,
while the moon brimmed with fire mined from the dark,
light finally freed of its mantle of rock.
It was numinous, perfect.

The Mary Block

Pleasure, for my great-great-grandmother,
was always deferred.
You'll get your reward in Heaven
the creed of her fellow Brethren
as they trod their narrow path towards
a stern, starch-collared God.
Abstinence deemed a virtue,
while hardship fell like blessings
on their heads.

Not that Mary never softened.
At times she pitied the wanting faces
of her offspring.
Scarlet ribbons … marbles … a waxen doll …
You'll get it when my ship comes in!
Almost a promise when you live by the harbour
of a city a-bristle with ships,
and surely not idle
(for Mary Block was never idle).

Unlike her daughters, sent out for pig's fry
but sidling along the quays in search of adventure
amongst the stacked timber, the bales of tobacco,
the casks of amber Bristol Milk,
and finding a ship gilded to legend
by a shadow-shuttered dawn,
the name *Mary Block* engraved on her bows
and escaping like orisons from their mouths
as they hallelujah up Christmas Steps
towards disappointment.

Hairshirt

In my beginning,
when all my life was written down,
today was ringed in red and set aside for walking,

from Holne to lonely Ryder's Hill,
where, on a clear day, you might see the spill of shore
from Portland to the distant Lizard.

I should be eating oranges beside a warrior's rocky cairn,
letting seeds of larksong trickle in my ears.
Instead, I'm wondering why I'm here

amongst these piles of plates and pans,
scrubbing sinks until they gleam
like Plymouth Sound.

Mill Tut

for TF

squats upon its haunches
like a creature giving birth
over the charred grist of a warrior chief,
and the weapons, meat and pots
his people leave with bleeding hands
and grief-shrammed hearts

upon the old, straight track
beneath the river bed of stars

crowned with frosted firs,
canopied with snow-thick cloud,
sleeps amid the shivering rowans
while fleet shadows cut and burn,
and mutter in their tongues
stories coppiced from the trees

through sacred wood and rock
the icy torrent carves its path

awakes to cannon crack
and the screams of shattered men,
neighbours, enemies, once friends,
slain and shovelled side by side
while their women's bellies swell
with the spoils of holy war

the windmill shepherds time,
grinds the centuries into days

settles back and yawns,
drowsing in the summer's still
as the river fingers wrappers,
silver beer tins, plastic bags,
and children paddle in the weir
on stones and broken glass

dreams of winter's king arisen,
striding song-filled from his grave

Mill Tut lies above the river Trym in Bristol. The site of a bronze-age
round barrow, it served for a time as a windmill stead. In the 1930s, two
cannonballs were unearthed nearby.

Night Feed

While he feeds,
starfish-fingered and sharkling-eyed,

she listens to the ocean in her ears
and longs for strong, hot tea,

wondering when it was – exactly –
that she turned into her mother

and the man alongside her
became another child,

to be indulged with sleep
and a blind eye.

Pasqueflower

In the dead time, between Christmas
and the first daffodils on the dresser,
the children long for snow.
From behind closed windows
they gaze on a world that is hollow
and grey as a dustbin,
willing whiteness into existence.
But the city lies low under brushstrokes of rain
that sweep up the channel from the sea,
glazing pavements and streets.

One day fat flakes, soft as breadcrumbs,
scatter themselves on the ground
in the thinnest of crusts.
For a moment there is snow.
The children plan their snowman.
But the rain's wash soaks its opalescence
and melts their fragile sculptures into tears.

So the velvet pelt of frost
that wraps the earth will have to do.
Their footprints map the landscape
as they creak across the grass,
exhaling the nap of the air.
And they look for the promise of spring
pushing up through the soil,
stroking silvery tufts of pulsatilla,
barely feathered as hatchlings
still wet from the egg.

Duplicity

Janus is dead.

She has eclipsed his eyes with pennies.
She has zipped his bloodless flesh in a bag and buried it.
She has painted her walls white.

Now his key slides in the lock.

He is as dangerous as buttercups
gilding their bane
at the turn of the stairs.

Prawle Point

Don't imagine for a moment
that I didn't think of you
just because the sun spilt honey
and the tumbling lanes drowsed,
mesmerised by flowers.
True, my memory tripped
like wind through wheat fields,
chasing Chinese whispers, wild rumours,

only to eddy on itself
as we stumbled down the blinded combe
towards your crucible of fleet, elusive dreams,
where, beyond a crest of hawthorn,
a cormorant kept the look-out
from its lonely pedestal.
Basalt angel? Reliquary urn?
My eyelid flickered in the glare.

Fifteen days ago we launched
your narrow, wooden boat.
Flags flapped low, taut wires and lines
against high masts tolled your passing.
And one black cardigan, forgotten,
lifted from a railing on the breeze,
as hapless – hopeless – as the sail
of the Athenians' homebound ship.

This Healing Hour

for HH

The children are asleep now,
and he is out. The dishwasher
drones in the distant kitchen,
the pages turn with tiny sighs.

In my mind's eye
the words blur into your face,
your broad hands, raw as scoured hams,
your swollen fingers.

You would have loved this healing hour,
the stalwart lamplight shouldering back
the faithless night,
the waiting day.

I see you
scribbling pencilled verse
on surplus scraps of greaseproof paper,
observing

eleven sets of nappies
flap and twist in the gritty wind
like luminous petals
of cyclamen blossom.

The Potter

Was it his dream landscape too,
that wooded combe
cut deep in moorland
under bleak, sheep-cobbled hills,
where every tree trunk, stump and rock
is wrapped and wound around with velvet,
like the inside of a casket
or a sumptuous padded cell
submerged in silence,
save the river
claiming innocents by name,
and all glazed green
bar bruise of bluebells
and amongst the starry mosses
something floating whitely up
through all the layers of sunken light,
the lustred air so atmospherically reflected
in this pot that just one touch
transports me there?

Or through some hairline crack in time
had he foreseen his drowning son, his daughter
spiralling through water,
while above them rolling combers
break … dissolve … obliterate?

*William Baron's Barnstaple pottery flourished from 1893 to 1935, when,
on a day-trip to Morwenstow, three family members were drowned, after
which he sold his business to his rival, C H Brannam.*

Meditation On A Bristol Tomb

Here you lie, as they say,
not dead but sleeping,
beside your stiffly coiffured goodwife
in your eternal marriage bed.

You and your two mediaeval brothers
manufactured covers.
The futures you invested in were chantries
to pray for your immortal souls.

I wonder what those woollen warmers were called
before you cornered the market?
Though I have to say,
these days you're looking stony cold.

So roll over and let me tuck you up,
Edmund Blanket.

*Flemish weaver Edmund Blanket died in 1371 and is buried in St
Stephen's Church, Bristol.*

The Red Of His Coat

Everyone she's loved has left,
their names and memories worn thin
and sloughed like skin,
even her husband of sixty-six years, whom
for these last few weeks she's known
by the red of his coat.

Now she's lying, stripped, transfixed,
a spilt reminiscence
glistening on her chin.
Only her hands are still alive:
they will not be held or tucked in tidily
by her sides,

but shape the space about her bed,
track the writhing of a pent
and coiling mind,
her tapered fingers pinched to heads
that sway and taste the freighted air
in search of threads,

a trace that might just shed
some light on this darkening room,
this waiting place that isn't home
with photographs of unknown faces,
all these cards and flowers brought
by weeping strangers.

Hefted

They moved northwards.
Fishermen, sailors in search of work,
abandoning homes, their salt-bitten villages,
freeing themselves from the tidal grip.
And farmhands
from orchards and meadows,
yeomen leaving their flocks
on the floating fields of the Levels.

They became chimney sweeps, railway workers,
purveyors of faggots in pails
to layers of tram lines.
And settled with locals –
folk who'd lived in this city
since before the days of the plague,
their forebears tumbled into pits
under the Horsefair.

As Bristolian as streets bristling with boats,
and the Nails, and that terminal –awl sound
that sticks in the back of our throats.
As in the definition of 'heft':
'ancestral areawl of sheep or goats',
that inherited memory of home
that drives them back to their habitat
over unknown countryside.

They have to be sold with the farm,
these flocks and herds
that fit like a jigsaw,
whose members know the lie of their land,
where it is safe to gambol and graze
and where the most treacherous mires are found;
lore passed down through generations
from dam to lamb or kid,

and still indigenous to our tribe
if our slide down the M5
south and west is anything
to go by,
our instincts magnetised like filings,
like starlings spun on glimmering wings
as they swarm and pour into the reed beds
in the season of singing trees.

Warning

to a diabetic daughter

You're headed again
for that distant city,
the one you had the temerity
to call 'home'.

It wasn't a slip of the tongue.

The outrage that I feigned
contained some truth,
though for the record I'll confess
pride in how you've made your way

even as I wrestle
with not knowing,
mornings awaiting your text
that says 'still alive'.

I'd thought your companion in check,

but now I've seen its naked face
upon your pillow.
Don't be fooled, my girl;
don't take it for your lover.

Persephone In Exile

Her hands are stained with glut:
cherries, plums made into jellies,
jam and chutney;

and apples, pears in layered paper;
onions plaited into swags
and hung to dry.

On the stove tomatoes simmer;
courgette slices stare from jars
like whitened faces.

And piles of pomegranate,
pulped to syrup sweetened
with a mother's love

that sticks and trickles down her fingers,
and blisters like hot silver
on her tongue.

And as she cuts from crown to base
to open up the flesh she's tasted,
she regrets her granite lover

in his cold, exacting halls,
the six seeds like bloody tears
she failed to eat.

New Found Land

When the poet has finished reading,
they decide to end the evening
in the bar that overlooks the floating harbour.
Outside the night is city dark,
the moon is curling
like a mussel in its shell,
with the river, black as absence,
swelling through its gritty heart.

She wants to talk of pictures painted,
Indian ice cream,
wind-blown rainbows,
and a steeple twisted into imagery.
He says the poet looks the same
as on TV.
Then he takes a sip of wine,
sets his drink down, and opines,

'You should have married somebody
who loves you.'

Through dazzled glass
she sees a ship slip past,
facsimile of Cabot's dream
that sailed across a mediaeval ocean,
its quest for gold and Asiatic spice
but only finding in their place
a misencountered, ice-bound
New Found Land.

This Serviceable Ghost

for William Morris

His overcoat is hanging
on the back of the north hall door,
as if he's somewhere in the house he loved,
bent over a manuscript, or drawing, or
listening to cows low
across the meadows.

It's not the mantle of a poet.
It doesn't swirl like John Ball's cassock
or Sigurd the Volsung's cloak.
This wrapping he swapped
for a box of unpolished oak
is the husk

of a grain of wheat,
crushed beneath the feet of mourners
at that rainy harvest home,
when beaten leaves dripped from pillars,
and lamps were ringed with
wreaths of oats and barley,

yet like the shed skin of a snake,
the case of a chrysalis discarded
once its earthly work is done,
this serviceable ghost of a great heart gone
earns its place now not through
usefulness but beauty.

Closer

They've grown closer
over years,
coupled in the kitchen
as she peels potatoes,
arms encompassing her waist,

his breath on her nape,
on the trace of sweat that sheens
her pliant skin, her soft
accommodation,

hand clasping
the hand that holds the knife,
guiding the blade.

Earth Stars

From the chronicles of trees
she wants monsters:

baleful Destroying Angels,
stellar brides of hell,
all innocence and virulence
in petticoats and veil,
or troops of gleaming Death Caps,
goose-stepping through leaves,
marshalling for massacre
in copses, killing fields, as if
escape clutched in her hand might gift
illusory control.

In forests damp and warm,
in thickets blanketed by spores,
the Prince with Devil's Fingers
knows their secret, loamy holes.
He can smell them, see them, feel them swelling
opening the ground,
thrusting through the litter
with a hungry, crackling sound.
He finds her Velvet Shanks and Blushers,
puts an Amethyst Deceiver in her hand.

In the sultry, starless dark,
she'll settle for a zodiac
of flesh and pearls and earth.

The Worm

Mary, 29th August 1784, aged 15

I knew she'd seen him again, knew it
the moment she walked through the door.
The light in her eyes was a flame
and her cheeks were burning
not with shame, but with stubble rash!
I tell you, she was afire with love!
Well, when I said I'd tell our mam
she went and grabbed me by the throat,
and hissed these very words right in my face.
She said 'I'd sooner die
than try to live without him!'

Jennet, 31st August 1784, aged 12

Friday last I caught her, rubbing her boots
with handfuls of pennywort leaves,
so when she walked up the path to church they'd squeak
and everyone would think they were brand new.
No one would have been fooled.
They all knew every stitch on her back
was four times handed down.
I suppose she found it growing
in some warm and sheltered spot.
Nothing clings to these bleak walls.
The boots I'd put back for winter we buried her in.

Ann, 31st March 1789, aged 45

Father said its lie was wrong, so like a lamb
all in a tangle, it couldn't be born. As for our mam,
well, she knew she was going to die.
I heard her cry and beg, she said
'If you can't help me, save the child!' The girl
she craved so badly, as helpmeet and as friend.
She'd tired of the company of men.
I was peeping through the crack in the door,
I saw them cut her belly open and lift her killer out.
Another brother.
That dark parcel handed to a suckling mother.

Thomas and Joseph, 17th May 1800, aged 23 and 14

I'd had a skinful, see? Soused as a mullet I was.
And too drunk to get out of bed,
so our Tom made young Joe go with him instead,
to help with the nets.
I was asleep when the storm roared in. Next thing
there was Father slamming his fist into the door,
and two naked corpses sprawled on the shore.
The sea might have stolen their lives, but it was
men from Llangennith who stripped them of dignity!
When the storm swallows them up,
it will come unbeknownst.

John, 7th July 1811, aged 38

There on the ground, that's where I found him,
by the light of the dying fire,
amongst the drunks and grinning women,
the mutton bones and cockle shells.
And by his side a sharpened stone
all caked with blood and hair.
He was barely alive.
I'd told him not to go, said he was mad
to head for Llangennith at Mabsant time.
For though the years ebb and flow without a trace,
bad blood leaves a dark and deepening stain.

John, 13th September 1824, aged 84

I never knew he'd kept her dress
till I found him slumped in his chair with it
pressed into his face,
no longer breathing a scent no longer there.
Come the end his sight had gone.
He'd blink and peer through milky eyes
and feel his way.
Not that it bothered him at all.
He seemed to find comfort in the dark.
Said he'd seen too much in his time
as it was.

Isaac, 5ᵗʰ July 1835, aged 47

The Old Worm is blowing.
The sea, the sands shift.
Trickle or pour, they all run out
over the heads of the drowning dead.
In the dunes a shard of stained glass.
On the floor of a nave
a censer in the shape of Jerusalem,
a knapped flint to whet the razor of a priest.
They sleep astounded.
These lost lives steeped in sand,
deaths set in stone.

In the churchyard of St Mary the Virgin, Rhossili, a gravestone lists the
deaths of the Griffith family. Here their stories are told by the next to die.

Survivors

for LRH

Your father, Somme survivor,
worked on a railway gang.
Word has it he was a hard man.

There are stories of him liking a drink, a bet,
picking wild flowers for the wife he kept
short of cash.
And of watching a kestrel arc and hang,
and drop on its prey like a train screams from a tunnel
and slices through flesh and bone.

You told me that story.
How they propped his mate against some sleepers
and waited for him to die.
Your father gave him a cigarette.
It must have been a familiar scene,
well worn as a greatcoat.

You went to the funeral. You were seven years old.
It seems strange to us, who ignore Death's existence
in case it's watching.

Later there were desert funerals
for soldiers of another war,
uprooted men, helpless as amputees, propped up
and waiting to die.
Mornings still as you wake, you shake
scorpions from your slippers.

The Ring

Where one ring used to sit,
a bitten imprint,
tight as the wire of a snare,
a private place laid bare
to sudden light.
Silvery onion skin,
thin, translucent
as dragonfly wings.

All things fly in time,
flesh will repair.
This fetch a wreath of breath
on frosted air.

Leap Day

Five and twenty past the hour
on a non-existent day
without a season.
An early evening rainstorm
chases molten silver mullions
down each westward-facing window.

For a while I watch it claw
the warp and weft of beaded gauze
blinding a scenery of tarmac, concrete, cloud.
There are landscapes in the rainlight:
glassy worlds meander
in a random stream,

encircle tumuli and earthworks
of a long-forgotten past;
snail trails
becoming frosted footpaths
over empty, unlit hills
from which a people with our faces

traced the swathes of ancient stars,
augurs of when to sow and reap.
I cannot wrap myself in their dreams,
only recognise and keep
a thread of memory
to make this weave complete.

Remedy

Numb stump of a thing in hibernation,
stilled beneath the ice of a quiet pond.
It didn't miss the light. It hadn't asked to be plucked
through her mouth and left
to crawl about like some dumb creature,
that feels but cannot think, that doesn't know
where it's supposed to be going.

Don't pick it up, don't touch it, don't carry it over the road
like a toad on a spade or in a kindly wheelbarrow.
Crush it, dry it, mummify it, and string it around her neck,
hang it over her pap, that vacant gap
where once it beat. And let it be a cure for contagion
or some other dread disease.
Let it be a remedy for love.

On Naxos

The embers of their fires
have long grown cold.
The sea reclaims its bounty,
now fish heads, guts and bones.
From the east the wind twists tripwires
out of sand, but it's too late:
empty scallops sail the tide line
like disappearing boats.

Why must you always trawl for love
in the parched heart of the dunes,
in the broken ties of bindweed
and the cryptic runes
that birds print on the shore?

Mute

for Jo G

The room is rapt, in silence,
unless the shepherding of air
makes a sound I cannot hear,
like the gasp of leaves in free-fall,
the shrill of flowers
as they are picked.

Words that filled my mouth
with their flavour
wither to husks,
stick in my throat.
I am mute
in this place of poems,

plucked from nothing
and given form
with a clap like a dove
starting into flight,
while my hands hang,
dumb lumps of meat.

In time
I might trace
that shimmer of purple,
conjure voice from empty space,
sign the infinite shape
the word poetry makes.

Redcliffe

In the poet's church,
already ancient,

centuries melt like candles,
slumber-coloured, honey-thick,

and swallow me in Lenten shadows,
seared by sulphurous daffodils,

where scorched lips in the wilderness
whisper their existence,

where parched hearts dully
drum the blood-beat

...breathe our breath ...

and fill me, like an unborn child
moored inside and tumbling,

a silver fish, glimpsed
through darkening waters,

and closer now
than those outside

whose seconds snap
like brittle bones.

The Coldest Spell

After he left,
the coldest spell
in twenty years.
Nine nights of snow,
and frost on the bed
she's sledged to the window.

There's salt on the path
and in her wounds.
She broods on the poet,
adrift in a winter
too distant for her
to remember,

cutting her vengeance
from fire and ice.
She is more Ancient Mariner
sailing her ship, her failure
heavy round her neck,
the waters dreamless.

And the bridge between them
closed to traffic
by icy spears that shatter glass.
He requests his driving licence.
She writes her blessing
behind the stamp.

Public Transport

Traffic stacked back up the hill;
the flash photography of sun
on rain-glossed pavements.
I am travelling incognito,
reading a book I have re-titled
'Do Not Disturb'.

Still a voice drags me off the page,
out of Carver's 'Afghanistan';
it's demanding
'Which stop is it for the bus station?
I've got to get to Nottingham
or some place miles from here!'

I force myself to answer
'I think it's the one after next',
and then, because I feel I have to,
'my sister lives near there',
but he's screaming 'I'm leaving before I kill her
or she kills me!'

Beyond the mirrored windscreens
starving Gothic arches roar above the Portakabins.
On College Green a camera crew is waiting
for news to happen
while the bus trundles inexorably
towards our stops.

The Gatekeeper

There's no one left to mourn them.
Only stony-faced angels keep watch
over the names of forgotten children,
written in lichen,
blotted with moss.

Flowers must bring themselves:
dandelions for Mary Kate;
stately cuckoo-pints for Diana,
the siren shine of malevolent berries
no longer a worry.

From the tower
the clock strikes four quarters and one.
A gatekeeper settles on a stone.
Its wings wear the colours of autumn fallen,
umber and rust.

A clatter of jackdaws comes bustling back,
tatters the death pall with tender talk.
Playground voices shoulder through oak trees,
boisterously singing
the Hokey-Cokey.

Small World

You claim that grasshoppers make their luck,
and today you rubbed your legs together
and hopped to the beach.
You saw dolphins in the Gulf,
turtles, pelicans, Louisiana herons.
Your face was basted in the Texan sun.

There's no need for you to tell me
that you've landed very well,
lodged in a cabin behind a bakehouse
owned by a woman who loves your songs
and whose passions are flowers called angel trumpets
and abandoned cats.

Now in the still of early dusk your door lies open.
The cats and the scent of exotic blooms
fill up your room.
A black Siamese is licking your hand,
you've washed your shirts,
and now you're heading out to eat.

And why (you add in afterthought)
don't I come with you to investigate
this alien, cicada-laden dark?
You're tired of being on your own
and though we're tourists, we'll be safe.
Your Belisha beacon face will light our way.

But here the April hail is rattling at the window.
The bars are closed, the restaurants
shuttered for the night.
You're six hours and five thousand miles away
as the heron flies,
and I should sleep.

Last night, you say, out of the blue
you chanced on somebody who came
from the same small factory town as I do.
She lived on the road that serves the air field
more than thirty years ago.
No, you don't know her name.

Danaë

for A P-K

It comes too late:
the realisation that her gilded suitor is not
what he seems.

That behind
the silken words he sings,
there is no song.

That underneath
his placid mask he wears
a mask.

When she looks,
there's no one lying beside her
in the mirror

but a fiery light
that sears her thighs
and the mad

cacophony
of ten thousand pennies
dropping.

Kin

Every November they gather together,
raggedy black with petroleum sheen
and sparks in their feathers.

Most live local,
drifting from suburbs like bonfire smoke,
although others hurl in from further afield,
storming up songlines,
until, like a genie freed from a lamp,
they swirl, and set the sky alight
with their crackling dance.

A parliament of starlings,
cacophonous cousins,
an argumentation of uncles and aunts!

Then one venerable elder
hunches his shoulders, opens his throat
and lets fly a hymn in notes
grown richer over years,
swelled by a hundred kindred voices,
all singing in different keys
their shared story.

Watchet

They've set the statue with its back to the sea,
so instead of the lighthouse at the mouth of the harbour,
the Ancient Mariner weighs the feathers of his shame.

Or is he trying to read the inscription,
which boldly makes the claim that Coleridge wrote his rime
inspired by trip to this spot?

We had a laugh at that:
the notion that this workaday port with its stolid boats
and the lurking smell of fish

might birth a tale of emerald ice-bergs,
of a painted ship on a painted sea, and Death
and red-lipped Life-in-Death, her skin as white as leprosy.

It's an equally imaginative leap,
or a cynical pitch for the more literary
sort of tourist.

Still, as we gaze from the harbour railing
at the greys of the sky and the greys of a sea
paling to pearled luminosity,

fleet swallows trail their streamers on the breeze,
and sing of dreams and stranger stories
from the oceanic plains of Africa.

Taking The Plunge

For you a seductress sea,
one that winks and glitters you in,
mouths your skin with kisses.
Yes, you'd prefer a warmer touch
but you keep your arms down by your sides,
you keep on walking till the sand slides
from your feet.

You can hear your siren's song,
she's perma-tanned and sun-bleached blonde.
You feel the glassy grip of current tug you free.
You're tasting salt now, salt and fish,
your blood is rising with the tide,
arms lift and fall like semaphore
only she will read.

And as she rolls you in her dance
your memories shard like glancing light,
they stream away like coloured bubbles
from your reach.
You leave your life,
old dreams, your family
folded in a pile upon the beach.

Sedgemoor

The final lunge of sunlight
in evening's falling green. A barn owl
hunts the serried hedgerows, the marching trees.

Skirl of white and skirmish. Night cries are cut short
by its heart-stopping
drop, the eternal mercy of drawn steel.

Sacrificial gifts of blood
for ghosts who moulder in this earth,
their murder fields.

The English Riviera

The sky has cried all morning,
drowning the sea.

As a child
I'd wait at this caravan window
for the hiss of Triumph Herald tyres,
for a rift in the cloud, for my nascent life
to happen.

Eventually you happened.

Now you're browning on a beach in Sardinia
with another
while I rust.
Would I sooner sit here,
waiting?

Probably.
Just.

Full Circle

In ancient China
the moon is made of figured silk,
woven with the pattern of galloping hares,
three conjoined by a single ear,
together whole.

An eternal circle
embroidered on bolts of cloth,
carried by camel through singing sands,
the booming dunes of wind-whipped
Xhiang Sha Wan,

where Silk Road
frays to quick oasis, and
wondering artists paint three hares
on sacred temple cavern walls.
The Buddha's wheel

of life and death
rolls through Persia's burning plains,
eclipses sere, salt-desert suns: a brazen tray
engraved with hares, a stamped,
Islamic copper coin.

Crossing rivers, bridging rifts
in hidden groves of moss and stone,
these three hares chased on Jewish tombs
and makeshift tabernacle roofs,
the blackened beams

of Dartmoor churches
at the edges of the earth, bear
a trinity of hares, three in one, the risen son,
beneath a moon that pins
the universal oceans.

*The enigmatic symbol of the three hares is found the length of the Silk
Road.*

Sleeping With The Enemy

For all that she is determined
not to slide,
not to waver,
not to make things easy for him,
she can't keep vigil
all the time,

and just as her mind
treads in worn footsteps,
just as his tongue calls her 'love'
at the end of a careless sentence,

each dawn is printed
with the spoor of a dream,
like the scent of fox, hot,
musky with the fear that asleep
she might yield some quarter
she can't remember.

That she might smile,
say, 'It doesn't matter.
No hard feelings.
Want some tea?'

That nineteen once more
she'll unslip some buttons,
and like a vixen in season,
summon him in.

A Falling Of Feathers

for ES

This morning, a falling of feathers:
death as a blessing on soundless wings.
I remembered
red feathers on crazy paving,
a ring dove, the leonine gleam
of a sparrowhawk's fixed eye.
A meeting with fate
on an urban savannah.
Two weeks later you nearly died.

This morning I found you in the kitchen.
This time you'd awakened,
partaken of manna to balance your blood.
While you rested,
I hefted this handful of feathers
against the other,
filled with life,
the feathers as soft and grey
as undefined horizons.

Poem For A Final Anniversary

We arrived the day before Yom Kippur.
Men in black on the shoreline
were watching the setting sun.
The moon was ours alone.

I'd carried it carefully with me,
wrapped in lingerie and blessings of confetti,
and I hung it over the painted sea
that kissed the periphery of our Promised Land,
its pale face as perfect
as a virgin honey jar.

We saw the Wailing Wall,
the Garden of Gethsemane,
we walked the Stations of the Cross
to crowded Calvary,
our Passion printed on the linen
of our trashed and tumbled bed.

When the time came to fly home
I bound our moon up in its folds.
Its sweetness seeped into your blood,
turning you to water,
till you dragged its sickly light beneath,
drowned it in your deeps,

stranding love upon the shore,
wrapped in funeral black,
an insect
trapped in amber.

Dragonfly

Easy rider in gleaming leathers,
twist of technicoloured wiring,
Aerial's entrails.

You should be tacking through slack waters,
hawking down your secret
beats and bridleways,

stitching pond and ditch together
with a thousand flying eyes,
a creel of hooks.

Not tumbled from the sky,
smashed and dead at this tidal edge,
turning to salt.

Far-fallen angel
whose dragnets trawled their hoard of shine
in leaded panes of rainbow light

now suddenly
frail as mourning lace
and funeral tapers.

The Hanging Gardens

Not sleek and sun-stroked, not today:
the sea a jar of dirty turpentine,
leached browns that rust to grey.

Beyond the shore, steep cliffs stare into mist,
raw-faced, the colour of old blood,
old loves
whose hearts and carved initials
melt in salt and spray,
or are erased in a sudden roar and falling.

Above the edge
the Sidmouth gardens hang
and cling to treasured things:
a fence a bracelet; crumpled walls silk scarves;
and summerhouses, sheds
discarded trinkets,

while on the sand a lost tree,
wrenched from loam,
blossoms unexpectedly with foam.

Wronged

I shall not be killing our children,
or sending your mistress a dress
embroidered with poison.
I'd sooner knit nettles into coats
and with stung fingers pluck love
from under a smother of feathers.

I shall not seek deathlessness through death,
or revenge in a vaporous breath
that draws me under winter's ice and snow.
I shall not be penning flayed poems
or prose: it seems
the market's been cornered in those.

I shall not be mislaying my mind
or drowning in melancholy songs
of love betrayed and squalid wrongs.
There's rue for you, but none for me.
I'm through with flowers and memories.
I'll weave my freedom in my hair.

Surtsey

'The hot stars down from Heaven are whirled.
Fierce grows the steam and the life-feeding flame,
Till fire leaps high about Heaven itself.'

I

After fire,
a mythic darkness.
Lava and ashes on black waters.
The suck and rattle of porous pebbles,
an unseen shore.
Pre-dawn greys. Then,
as daybreak makes its landfall,
the fissured rift of scouring sun,
the wind's thin blade.
Cracked salt,
a barren, toppling cliff.
We shield our eyes against the glare.

II

Talismans and magic
were no use:
holed stones threaded with red ribbon,
heart-shaped pebbles,
amulets of sea-washed glass.
Tinfoil stars failed to slay the shadow,
banish malice from our hall.

Bloodless And Boneless
Behind The Door.
Home is the hunter
with his bag of barbs
and scorn.

III

They will come over water,
coursing cold, salt currents
of wind and sea.
A flotilla of possibility
in the gizzards and feathers
of guillemots and soaring fulmars,
on splinters of driftwood
and grassy tussocks
washed ashore.
Doughty traffickers in hope,
seeding bare and broken folds
of frozen stone.

Clearing From The West

Dissolution of cliffs in mist,
as if the sea has risen up to swallow
the headland, the drowning fields.
This rain would wall us in all morning,
though the forecaster predicts a gradual
clearing from the west

as the headlights haul themselves upstream
through the falling sky,
leaving behind huddled cottages,
sodden thatch, bespattered livestock,
picking its way
through a sump of mud,

to where the sullen moor's clenched knuckles
break the grey. And though we've been told,
it's still a miracle:
spindrift of sunlight igniting gorse candles,
drawing the river with silver threads
over boulders.

Cloud-clumped sheep scud at our passing,
streaming ponies scatter rainbows
from their manes.
In puddled ruts like shiny portholes,
the earth throws back a sky
I could reach out and touch.

The Wedding Tree

In autumn
she huddles old bones
against equinoctal storms,
discards a parsimonious harvest
of tarnished pears with crackled skin,
fit only for starlings.
A crabbed munificence

I've forgotten
in this ragged April dawn
as she spreads her blossom-clotted arms,
as white,
as mad as Miss Havisham's ghost,
and strips herself of wedding petals
at the insistence of the wind.

Watered silk and crimson seed,
throughout this Easter perfumes
bleed into my days,
and in a blessing of confetti
I am purified of love, and rise,
a bride to the remainder
of my life.

Iago

'Demand me nothing. What you know, you know.'

I

The dead dogs are starting to stink
forty years after the fact:
the trespasser with its throat torn out;
the family pet
bludgeoned, drowned
in the swimming pool.

Blood in the gutter,
drifting through water,
failed to stain the angel
child with the pointed chin,
fair hair, white hat,
a blinding smile.

Spectral dogs
footstep my dreams,
red-eyed in bristling, brute terror
but it's the glee
in your recollection
that hounds me.

II

After the wedding presents
I'll unwrap you.
Peel off your sheath of shantung silk,
your flimsy lingerie.
Then, when you are naked,

when I've got you
where I want you,
I'll shine a light upon you
as methodically, assiduously
I strip you,

paying attention
to that tenderest of spots
between your ears,
rendering service to your need,
wielding my whetted silver tongue

exquisitely.
I shall dismantle you and smile
You will not notice how.
I'll only hurt you
as much as you allow.

III

You will not grow gills.
Breathing will always feel like swallowing knives.
Those iron arms around your chest,
so strict your heart might burst,
will never rust.

A tonnage of marble and suds,
yet with the slowing of body and blood comes
acceptance.
Your mind will close
like a sea anemone in deep shade,
tucking away exploratory fronds,
those questing red and purple feelers of enquiry.

Sometimes you might glimpse
a gaslit face, an intimation
of your sunk and shrunken self,
tarnished, with darkness in your eyes,
a fractured mirror.
Or a reminder of your life:
rippled sand a furrowed field,
shoals of silvery sand eels flickering,
like whitebeam leaves in luminescent summer.

But mostly you'll forget.
Amnesia eases the worst hurting
with poultices of salt.

IV

Words were my protection,
written in silver around my wrist,
and the one that came unbidden
from the place that locks awareness
out of reach.

The pantomime is over.
All our straw is spun to fool's gold.
For now I recognise your name,
I see your lack,
the mark of Cain,

your father's hand
lying on your shoulder.
The diamond love you ground away
was only ever dishclout grey
to you.

A Moon Like This

You've called it a day.
Decided to settle
for a walk in the park
with the dog at twilight.
And this, you tell your dog,
will be enough.
And for a while it is
until, above the lollipop trees,
a lunatic moon hurls herself
in the sky's blue well.
A tuppenny bit to wish on,
and a small wind rises,
riffles your blood.
You clear your throat,
it makes no sound,
but another night,
on a moon like this,
you might hear yourself
howling.

Indigo Dreams Publishing
132, Hinckley Road
Stoney Stanton
Leicestershire
LE9 4LN
www.indigodreams.co.uk

Papers used by Indigo Dreams are recyclable products made from wood grown in
sustainable forests following the guidance of the Forest Stewardship Council.